The Four Seasons

"Le Quattro Stagioni"

D1304061

ANTONIO VIVALDI
Arranged by R. FRED KERN

CONTENTS

Alfred

The Four Seasons

"Le quattro Stagioni"

Theme from "Spring" Op. 8, No. 1

Movt. I

Antonio Vivaldi
Arranged by R. Fred Kern

Theme from "Summer" Op. 8, No. 2

Movt. I

Antonio Vivaldi
Arranged by R. Fred Kern

Theme from "Autumn" Op. 8, No. 3

Movt. I

Antonio Vivaldi
Arranged by R. Fred Kern

Theme from "Winter" Op. 8, No. 4

Movt. II

Antonio Vivaldi
Arranged by R. Fred Kern